R0083171025

05/20

FunKY
Fractions

Lisa Arias

Rourke
Educational Media

rourkeeducationalmedia.com

Scan for Related Titles
and Teacher Resources

Before Reading:

Building Academic Vocabulary and Background Knowledge

Before reading a book, it is important to tap into what your child or students already know about the topic. This will help them develop their vocabulary, increase their reading comprehension, and make connections across the curriculum.

1. *Look at the cover of the book. What will this book be about?*
2. *What do you already know about the topic?*
3. *Let's study the Table of Contents. What will you learn about in the book's chapters?*
4. *What would you like to learn about this topic? Do you think you might learn about it from this book? Why or why not?*
5. *Use a reading journal to write about your knowledge of this topic. Record what you already know about the topic and what you hope to learn about the topic.*
6. *Read the book.*
7. *In your reading journal, record what you learned about the topic and your response to the book.*
8. *After reading the book complete the activities below.*

Content Area Vocabulary
Read the list. What do these words mean?

commutative property of
     multiplication
convert
denominator
factor
greatest common factor
improper fraction
mixed number
numerator
reciprocal
simplify

After Reading:

Comprehension and Extension Activity

After reading the book, work on the following questions with your child or students in order to check their level of reading comprehension and content mastery.

1. *Why do we need to change mixed numbers to improper fractions when multiplying and dividing fractions? (Asking questions)*
2. *Why do whole numbers have a denominator of 1 in fraction form? (Asking questions)*
3. *Explain KCF. (Summarize)*
4. *Why should you simplify fractions before you multiply? (Asking questions)*
5. *What is a reciprocal? (Summarize)*

Extension Activity

Practice multiplying and dividing fractions with playing cards! You will need a deck of playing cards, paper, and pencil. Draw four cards from the deck. Arrange those four cards into two fractions. Now multiply and divide the fractions. Remember the rules for multiplying and dividing fractions. Continue practicing until you finish the deck. Once completed you can shuffle and repeat!

TABLE OF CONTENTS

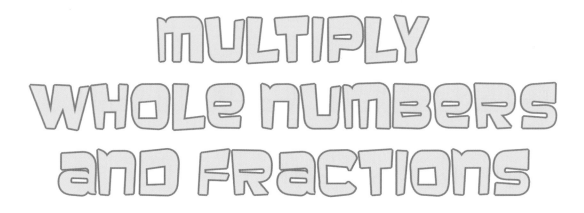

MULTIPLY WHOLE NUMBERS and FRACTIONS

Multiplying by whole numbers greater than one
is something that we have always done.

$$4 \times 6 = 24$$

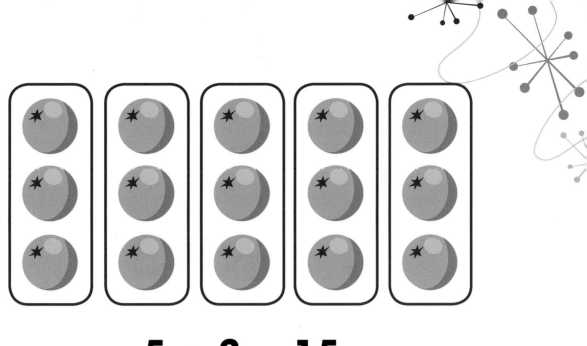

5 × 3 = 15

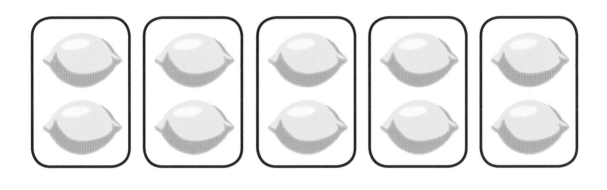

5 × 2 = 10

It is easy to see that the **product** becomes a larger number quite nicely.

Multiplying by Fractions Models

Now it is time to stop and think
how fractions cause products to shrink.

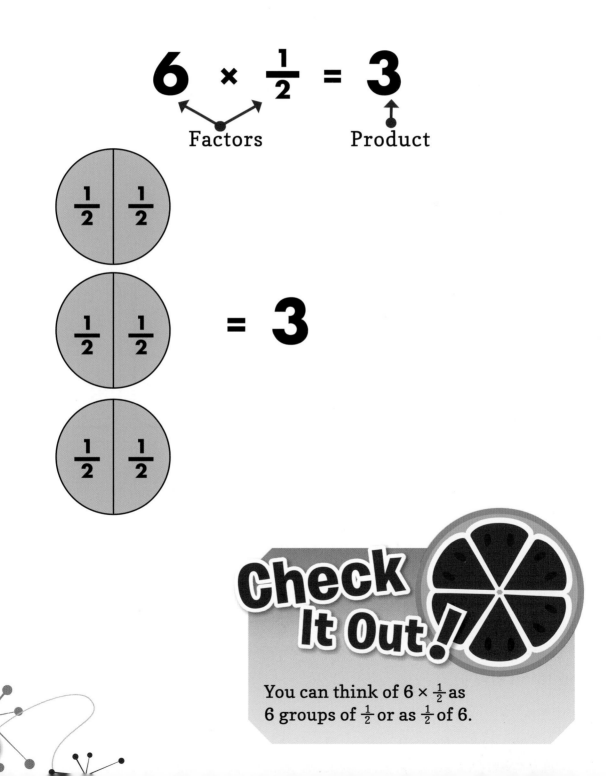

$$6 \times \frac{1}{2} = 3$$

Factors   Product

$$= 3$$

Check It Out!

You can think of $6 \times \frac{1}{2}$ as
6 groups of $\frac{1}{2}$ or as $\frac{1}{2}$ of 6.

Products get even smaller when both factors are fractions.

$$\frac{1}{6} \times \frac{1}{2} = \frac{1}{12}$$

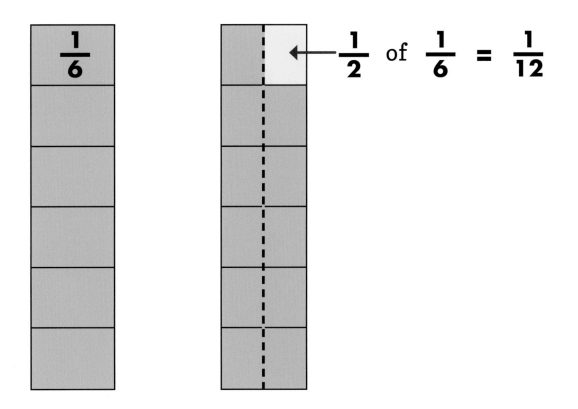

$$\frac{1}{2} \text{ of } \frac{1}{6} = \frac{1}{12}$$

Multiply Whole Numbers and Fractions

Repeated addition is helpful to see how multiplying works so perfectly.

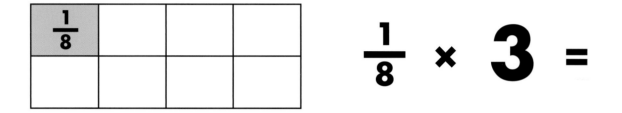

$$\frac{1}{8} \times 3 =$$

Add together 3 groups of $\frac{1}{8}$

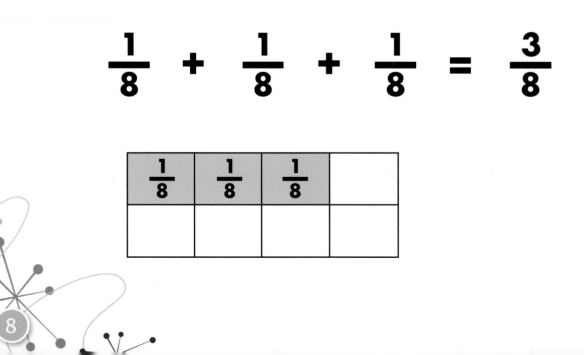

$$\frac{1}{8} + \frac{1}{8} + \frac{1}{8} = \frac{3}{8}$$

Repeated addition works just fine, but after a while,
simply multiplying becomes the style.

Before you begin, rewrite the whole number in fraction form by
placing the number over one.

$$\frac{1}{8} \times 3 \qquad \frac{1}{8} \times \frac{3}{1}$$

Next, multiply the numerators.

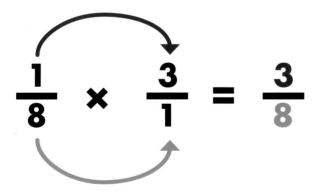

$$\frac{1}{8} \times \frac{3}{1} = \frac{3}{8}$$

Finally, multiply the denominators.

SIMPLIFY BEFORE YOU MULTIPLY

Always **simplify** before taking action on fractions. This is very helpful to do, so that the fractions are in simplest form for me and you.

To simplify, divide the **numerator** and **denominator** by their greatest common **factor** and you are through.

$$\frac{24}{32}$$ ←——• Numerator

←——• Denominator

24: 1, 2, 3, 4, 6, ⑧, 12, 24

32: 1, 2, 4, ⑧, 16, 32

8 is the Greatest Common Factor of **24** and **32**

$$\frac{24 \div 8}{32 \div 8} = \frac{3}{4}$$

Check It Out!

The **greatest common factor** (GCF) is the largest factor that two or more numbers share. List the factors of each number, no matter how small and pick the largest common factor of them all.

Simplifying Crisscross Style

Thanks to the **commutative property of multiplication**, when multiplying fractions you can simplify either numerator and denominator pair.

Divide by the GCF of 4 and 8.

$4 ÷ 4 = 1$ $\dfrac{1}{4} \times \dfrac{8}{1}$ $8 ÷ 4 = 2$

Divide by the GCF of 6 and 9.

$6 ÷ 3 = 2$ $\dfrac{6}{7} \times \dfrac{4}{9}$ $9 ÷ 3 = 3$

After simplifying either numerator and denominator pair, multiply the new numerators and the new denominators, fair and square.

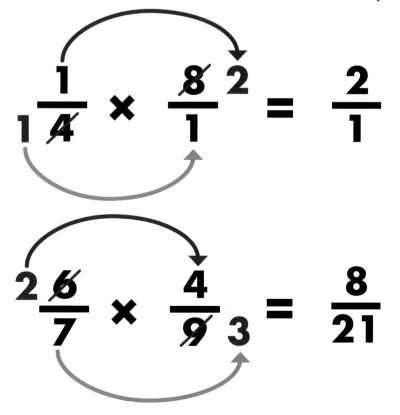

$$\dfrac{1}{4} \times \dfrac{8}{1} = \dfrac{2}{1}$$

$$\dfrac{6}{7} \times \dfrac{4}{9} = \dfrac{8}{21}$$

Step-by-Step Solutions

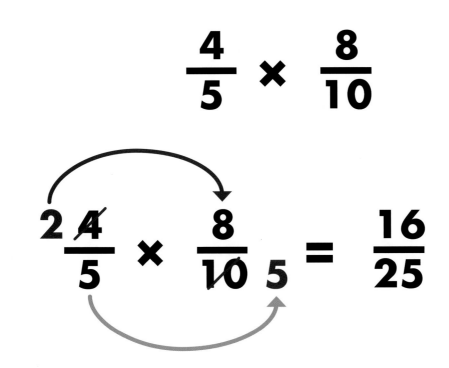

$$\frac{4}{5} \times \frac{8}{10}$$

$$2\frac{4}{5} \times \frac{8}{10}5 = \frac{16}{25}$$

Step 1: *Crisscross Simplify*

Divide 4 and 10 by their GCF 2.

4 ÷ 2 = 2
10 ÷ 2 = 5

Step 2: *Multiply numerators and denominators.*

2 × 8 = 16
5 × 5 = 25

$$\frac{2}{12} \times \frac{8}{7}$$

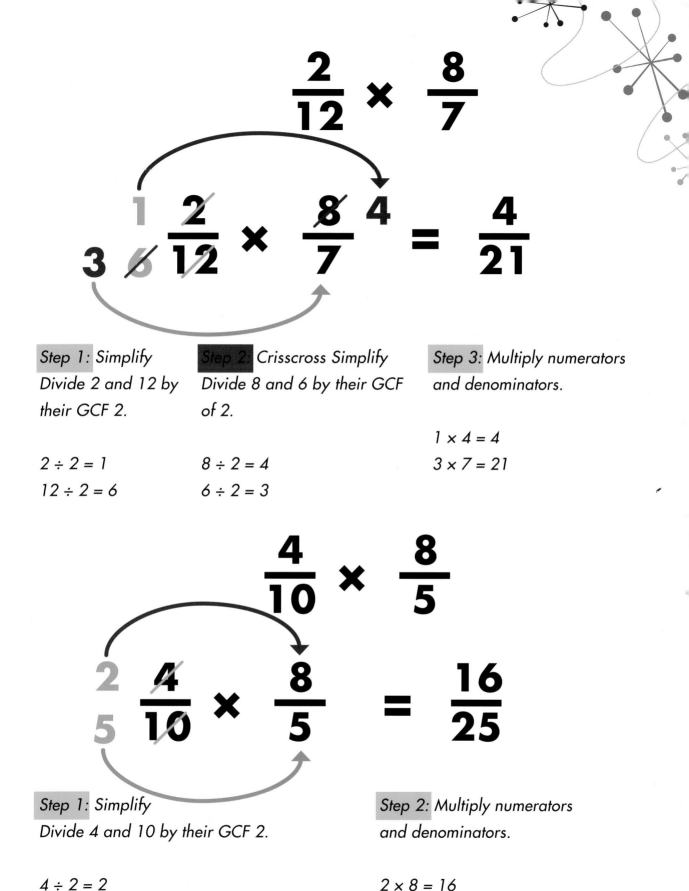

$$\overset{1}{\underset{3}{}} \frac{2}{12} \times \frac{8}{7}^{4} = \frac{4}{21}$$

Step 1: Simplify
Divide 2 and 12 by
their GCF 2.

Step 2: Crisscross Simplify
Divide 8 and 6 by their GCF
of 2.

Step 3: Multiply numerators
and denominators.

$2 \div 2 = 1$
$12 \div 2 = 6$

$8 \div 2 = 4$
$6 \div 2 = 3$

$1 \times 4 = 4$
$3 \times 7 = 21$

$$\frac{4}{10} \times \frac{8}{5}$$

$$\overset{2}{\underset{5}{}} \frac{4}{10} \times \frac{8}{5} = \frac{16}{25}$$

Step 1: Simplify
Divide 4 and 10 by their GCF 2.

Step 2: Multiply numerators
and denominators.

$4 \div 2 = 2$
$10 \div 2 = 5$

$2 \times 8 = 16$
$5 \times 5 = 25$

13

Improper Fractions as Mixed Numbers

If you find an **improper fraction**
after your multiplication is complete,
rename it as a **mixed number** nice and neat.
Take it one step at a time,
and your answer will be just fine!

Improper fractions happen when the numerator is larger than the denominator.

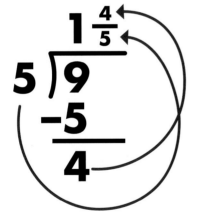

To convert, divide the numerator by the denominator. The remainder becomes the new numerator and the denominator remains.

$$\frac{9}{5} = 1\frac{4}{5}$$

Convert each improper fraction to a mixed number.

$$\frac{8}{3}$$

$$\frac{16}{5}$$

$$\frac{19}{8}$$

$$\frac{27}{7}$$

Mixed Numbers as Improper Fractions

If multiplying with mixed numbers ever appears,
you must take action and change it to an improper fraction.

Multiply the whole number
by the denominator.

Multiply.

Then add.

Add the numerator to your answer.

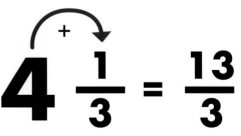

This becomes your numerator and
the denominator stays the same.

Change each mixed number to an improper fraction.

$$2\frac{5}{6}$$

$$4\frac{3}{8}$$

$$3\frac{5}{9}$$

$$6\frac{4}{7}$$

Multiply Mixed Numbers

Always multiply mixed numbers as improper fractions.

To convert, multiply and add.

$$1 \tfrac{1}{2} \times 2 \tfrac{1}{5} =$$

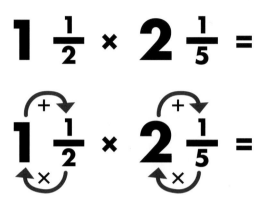

Simplify as needed, then multiply numerators and denominators.

$$\frac{3}{2} \times \frac{11}{5} = \frac{33}{10}$$

Convert your answer back to a mixed number in simplest form.

$$10 \overline{)33} \quad \begin{array}{r} 3\tfrac{3}{10} \\ \hline 33 \\ -30 \\ \hline 3 \end{array} \quad = 3 \tfrac{3}{10}$$

Multiply as improper fractions and answer in simplest form.

$$\frac{1}{3} \times 1\frac{3}{4}$$

$$1\frac{7}{8} \times 3\frac{1}{3}$$

$$2\frac{1}{7} \times 1\frac{1}{5}$$

$$\frac{1}{2} \times 8\frac{1}{3}$$

DIVIDE FRACTIONS

$$4 \div \frac{1}{2} = \,?$$

Count how many groups of $\frac{1}{2}$ are in 4?

Dividing whole numbers by fractions splits the whole number into smaller parts, creating an answer that is larger than it was from the start.

$$4 \div \frac{1}{2} = 8$$

How many groups of $\frac{2}{6}$ are in $\frac{5}{6}$?

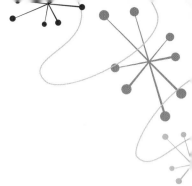

$\frac{5}{6}$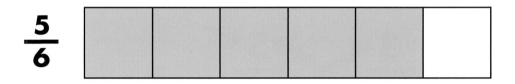

$\frac{2}{6}$

Reciprocals

Dividing fractions by the **reciprocal** is how things are done. Let's take some time for some reciprocal fun.

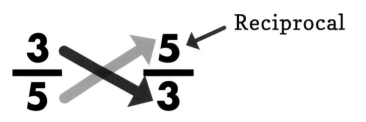

To find a reciprocal of a fraction, the numerator and denominator flip spots.

If you are finding the reciprocal of a whole number, change it to a fraction by placing the number over one.

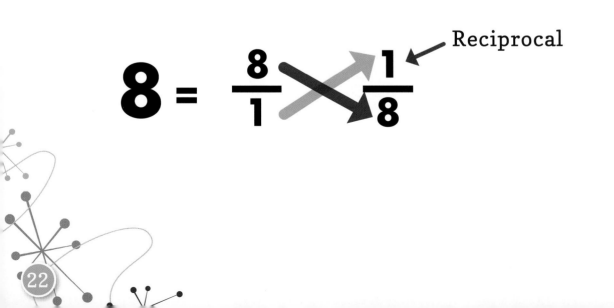

Check It Out!

Multiplying reciprocals is great fun because they will always equal one.

$$\frac{1}{1} \frac{3}{4} \times \frac{4}{3} \frac{1}{1} = 1$$

Divide Whole Numbers and Fractions

Before you begin, change the whole number to a fraction by placing it over one.

To divide, multiply the first fraction by the reciprocal of the second fraction.

Use KCF to remember each step.

K: *Keep the first fraction as is.*

C: *Change the division sign to multiplication.*

F: *Flip the last fraction to its reciprocal.*

After the steps are complete, keep things neat and simplify before and after you multiply.

$$6 \div \frac{2}{3}$$

$$\frac{^3\cancel{6}}{1} \times \frac{3}{\cancel{2}\,_1} = \frac{9}{1}$$

K   C   F

Divide and answer in simplest form.

$$15 \div \frac{5}{9}$$

$$6 \div \frac{3}{11}$$

$$4 \div \frac{1}{2}$$

$$8 \div \frac{4}{5}$$

Divide Fractions by Fractions

When dividing fractions by fractions, multiply the first fraction by the reciprocal of the second fraction.

Use KCF to remember each step.

K: *Keep the first fraction as is.*

C: *Change the division sign to multiplication.*

F: *Flip the last fraction to its reciprocal.*

After the steps are complete, keep things neat and simplify before and after you multiply.

$$\frac{5}{6} \div \frac{2}{3}$$

$$\frac{5}{\overset{2}{\cancel{6}}} \times \frac{\overset{1}{\cancel{3}}}{2} = \frac{5}{4} = 1\frac{1}{4}$$

K   C   F

Divide and answer in simplest form.

$$\frac{2}{7} \div \frac{3}{4}$$

$$\frac{4}{5} \div \frac{8}{9}$$

$$\frac{1}{6} \div \frac{4}{7}$$

$$\frac{5}{8} \div \frac{1}{3}$$

Divide Mixed Numbers

When dividing mixed numbers is near, never take action
until you convert each mixed number to an improper fraction.

Once your improper fractions are set, multiply the first fraction by the
reciprocal of the second fraction.

Use KCF to remember each step.

K: *Keep the first fraction as is.*

C: *Change the division sign to multiplication.*

F: *Flip the last fraction to its reciprocal.*

After the steps are complete, keep things neat and simplify before
and after you multiply.

$$5\frac{5}{8} \div 2\frac{1}{2}$$

$$\frac{45}{8} \div \frac{5}{2}$$

$$\frac{\cancel{45}^{9}}{\cancel{8}_{4}} \times \frac{\cancel{2}^{1}}{\cancel{5}_{1}} = \frac{9}{4} = 2\frac{1}{4}$$

K   C   F

Divide and answer in simplest form.

$$7\frac{1}{2} \div \frac{1}{2}$$

$$3\frac{3}{4} \div 5\frac{5}{8}$$

$$11\frac{1}{4} \div \frac{3}{4}$$

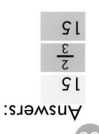

GLOSSARY

commutative property of multiplication (kuh-MYOO-tuh-tiv PROP-ur-tee uhv muhl-tuh-pli-KEY-shuhn): if the order of the factors change, the product remains the same

convert (kuhn-VURT): to change one number into another of equal value

denominator (di-NOM-uh-nay-tor): the bottom number of a fraction that shows the number of equal parts of the whole

factor (FAK-tur): the number or numbers that are multiplied

greatest common factor (GRAYT-esst KOM-uhn FAK-tur): the largest number that is a common factor of two or more numbers together

improper fraction (im-PROP-ur FRAK-shuhn): when a numerator of a fraction is larger than the denominator

mixed number (MIKST NUHM-bur): a number containing a fraction and whole number

numerator (NOO-muhr-a-tur): the top number in a fraction

reciprocal (ri-SIP-ruh-kuhl): a set of numbers whose product equals one

simplify (SIM-pluh-fye): to reduce a fraction to its lowest term

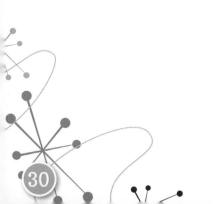

INDEX

WEBSITES TO VISIT

www.mathplayground.com/fractions_mult.html

www.math-play.com/Multiplying-Fractions-Millionaire/Multiplying-Fractions-Millionaire.html

www.aaamath.com/fra66ox2.htm

about the author

Lisa Arias is a math teacher who lives in Tampa, Florida with her husband and two children. Her out-of-the-box thinking and love for math guided her toward becoming an author. She enjoys playing board games and spending time with family and friends.

Meet The Author!
www.meetREMauthors.com

www.rourkeeducationalmedia.com

PHOTO CREDITS: Cover: © Talshiar, RussellTate

Edited by: Jill Sherman

Cover and Interior design by: Tara Raymo

Library of Congress PCN Data

Funky Fractions: Multiply and Divide / Lisa Arias
(Got Math!)
 ISBN 978-1-62717-717-7 (hard cover)
 ISBN 978-1-62717-839-6 (soft cover)
 ISBN 978-1-62717-952-2 (e-Book)
Library of Congress Control Number: 2014935594

Printed in the United States of America, North Mankato, Minnesota

Also Available as:

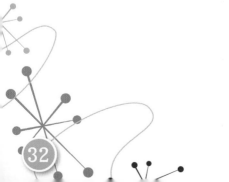